At One with JESUS

Rediscovering the Secret of Lectio Divina

Clifford E. Bajema

CRC Publications
Grand Rapids, Michigan

Unless otherwise indicated, the Scripture quotations in this publication are from the HOLY BIBLE, NEW INTERNATIONAL VERSION, © 1973, 1978, 1984, International Bible Society. Used by permission of Zondervan Bible Publishers.

At One with Jesus © 1998 by CRC Publications, 2850 Kalamazoo Ave. SE, Grand Rapids, MI 49560.

All rights reserved. With the exception of brief excerpts for review purposes, no part of this book may be reproduced in any manner whatsoever without written permission from the publisher.

Printed in the United States of America on recycled paper. ♻
1-800-333-8300

Library of Congress Cataloging-in-Publication Data
Bajema, Clifford E., 1941-
    At one with Jesus: rediscovering the secret of lectio divina / Clifford E. Bajema.
      p.   cm.
    ISBN 1-56212-354-8 (alk. paper)
    1. Spirituality—Biblical teaching. 2. Bible. N.T. John XVII—Study and teaching. 3. Bible—Reading. 4. Bible—Devotional use. I. Title.
BS2615.6.S65B34   1998
226.5'06—dc21   98-23651
                                                          CIP

10 9 8 7 6 5 4 3 2 1

Contents

Introduction 5

Session One: Glorify Yourself in Me (John 17:1-5, 10, 22) 11

Session Two: Finish Your Work in Me (John 17:4, 6-8) 19

Session Three: Pray for Me (John 17:9) 27

Session Four: Keep Me and Guard Me (John 17:11-15) .37

Session Five: Abide with Me—in the World (John 17:14-16, 18) 45

Session Six: Consecrate Me—in Truth and Love (John 17:17-26) 53

Bibliography 61

Introduction

Spiritual formation is much more than the accumulation of religious information. It shapes us into the image of Christ and moves us from one degree of glory to another. Spiritual formation allows us to behold the face, to become the place, and to be made the space of Christ. It helps us to become the body of Christ. In Hebrew thinking, the body represents the self in action. To become formed as the body of Christ is to become the face, the place, and the space where Christ reveals himself, shows his character, and manifests his glory.

Spiritual formation closely resembles physical exercise. It takes discipline, training, and endless repetitions in the gymnasium of holiness. Spiritual growth is hard work. It isn't all fun and good feelings. It can be boring and tedious. Sometimes it isn't supported by positive emotional confirmation. At times it requires the dogged determination of obedience.

LECTIO DIVINA

Ancient monastic Christians practiced a training method to help them remain consistent in their pursuit of holiness. This method taught them that in spiritual formation, discipline is the mother of spontaneity. In other words, holiness eventually comes more spontaneously and naturally to spiritual trainees who keep working at it, because they never delude themselves into thinking they have arrived. This training method—or spiritual discipline—used by the ancients was called *lectio divina*, translated loosely as *divine reading*.

Eugene Peterson, popular Christian author and professor of spiritual theology at Regent College in Vancouver, Canada, has written a very helpful essay on this discipline called "Caveat Lector" ("Let the Reader Beware"). Many of the insights in this introduction come from that excellent essay.

Lectio divina is a unified discipline with four connected stages: reading *(lectio)*, meditation *(meditatio)*, prayer *(oratio)*, and contemplation *(contemplatio)*. Rather than being consecutive stages, they are "elements thrown together in a kind of playful dance" (Peterson).

Unlike Protestants, Roman Catholic and Christian Orthodox believers have maintained this discipline in some form in their contemporary faith communities. Mainline, evangelical, charismatic, and Reformed Protestants would benefit greatly from taking this ancient discipline more seriously.

Unfortunately, many of us never give ourselves the opportunity to experience the spiritual blessings that come with proceeding beyond the reading *(lectio)* of God's Word. We assume that reading, studying, sermonizing, teaching, and praying briefly before or after our reading is enough.

Maybe the reason for this omission is that we fear meditation. It sounds too mystical, too subjective, too open to abuse by our imagination. These dangers certainly exist, especially if our meditation is cut off from the discipline of study that methods such as *lectio divina* incorporate. But reading without meditation can be just as dangerous as meditation without reading, for then the Word of God is merely intellectualized; it never makes the journey from our head to our heart. Biblical scholars especially must be careful to avoid this separation. Knowing God is not just knowing *about* God. As in C. S. Lewis's *Narnia* tales, the written and spoken Word of God is meant to be a "wardrobe" of entry into the wondrous world of God.

Another reason for the omission of meditation is time pressure. Meditation takes time—a whole lot of time. We have to slow down to meditate. Children have wonderfully active imaginations because they have plenty of time. They are not yet on the treadmill of taking care of urgent business. They are not tyrannized by the urgent. That explains why Lewis wrote his *Narnia* tales for children. It seems that too many of us adults have allowed our imagination to atrophy.

AN OUTLINE OF THE DISCIPLINE

Here is an outline of the discipline of *lectio divina*.

Stage One: Reading (lectio)

Lectio is entering the written and spoken Word of God by reading, prayer for illumination, study, and memorization. It's more than a surface reading. It is a deeply personal reading that moves beyond inductive study, which gathers facts, and deductive study, which "reasons out" our faith.

While *lectio divina* involves more than these, induction and deduction are certainly important elements. Through induction (asking who, what, when, where, why, and how questions) we gather information and accurate observations about the Scripture text. Through deduction (drawing rational conclusions) we arrive at principles and learn important lessons.

Lectio involves the exercise of what Richard Foster identifies as the more particular spiritual discipline of study. We might use dictionaries, concordances, commentaries, and other aids to get at what the text says. The goal of our study is *ex*egesis—reading out of the text what it actually intends to say. Our goal is not *eis*egesis—reading into the text what we want to hear. Says Peterson, "It is God's Word, and so we better get it right. Exegesis is the care we give to getting the words right. . . . Which is to say, the more spiritual we become—that is, the more personally God-attentive and Spirit-responsive we become—the more care we must expend on exegesis" ("Caveat Lector," *Crux*, March 1996, pp. 5-6).

Lectio may also involve speaking with a spiritual director or a mentor about the text, receiving instruction, or listening to a sermon.

However we engage Scripture at this level, we should always accompany our reading of it with a prayer for illumination. We depend on the voice of God to speak through the Word and to make it living and active.

To read well, we need to read slowly and repetitively so that we comprehend. A wonderful aid to comprehension is memorization. In Deuteronomy 6, God commands the

Israelites to write his Word on their hearts, as well as on their hands, their foreheads, their doorposts and even their gates.

Stage Two: Meditation (meditatio)

In the tales of C. S. Lewis, the written Word of God is the wardrobe of entry into Narnia, the mysterious, wondrous world of God. But the wardrobe is not Narnia. The written Word is not the world itself. As Eugene Peterson writes: "the written word is always less than the spoken word" ("Caveat," p. 5). The full experience of God is yet to come.

Knowledge of Scripture is necessary for religious meditation. But by itself it is not enough. When we enter the Word of God through reading, study, and memorization, we can look farther ahead. We anticipate entering the world of God through our imagination, through reflection, through spiritual breathing (inhalation of the Spirit and exhalation of sin and self), and through empathic listening.

Meditation allows us to go beyond information to inspiration, beyond observation to evaluation, beyond memorization to imagination. The grazer must become a salivator and a chewer. Left to themselves, fresh ground coffee beans do not make a good cup of coffee. They must percolate and brew. That's a slow process, as we know all too well when we're hovering over a brewing pot. Meditation is a listening, smelling, imagining, and waiting process.

Meditation helps us experience the grace of mystical union with the tri-unity of God. Through silent and secret musing, through listening to the inner whisperings of God in our hearts, we *take care of* our spirits. This is the literal meaning of "to meditate" in Greek and in Hebrew. As Brother Lawrence has said, in meditation we exercise ourselves in godliness. We practice the presence of God (*The Practice of the Presence of God*, p. 36). Psalm 119:15 gives us a typical example from the Bible: "I meditate on your precepts and consider your ways."

Stage Three: Prayer (oratio)

When we have entered the written and spoken Word of God through reading, and the world of God through meditation, we have not automatically come into the presence of Jesus Christ, the eternal Word of God. Jesus warned the Pharisees, "You diligently study the Scriptures because you think that by them you possess eternal life. These are the Scriptures that testify about me, yet you refuse to come to me to have life" (John 5:39-40).

God wants to have fellowship with us through the Word. He wishes to connect with us, to be in covenant with us, to meet us in worship. Prayer is the way to engage ourselves with God, to communicate with God in a two-way conversation. Prayer is a dialogue, not a monologue. It includes speaking and listening. Mysteriously, when we say in prayer what we have studied, memorized, and meditated on in God's Word, this same Word becomes the answer to our prayer. It comes back into our listening and praying hearts as a living, transforming, personal Word. God speaks. God directs, guides, convicts, illumines, forgives, and comforts us. This is the other side of prayer, the other side of the dialogue. Such prayers can be written down or journaled, making them part of the treasury of the prayers of the saints to which the church devotes itself in years to come.

Stage Four: Contemplation (contemplatio)

Contemplation is a lifestyle guided by the other three aspects of *lectio divina* (reading, mediation, and prayer). When we have entered into the written Word, into the world of God, and into communion with Christ, the Word of God in person, then we are ready for the Word to enter into our everyday lives. We are ready to experience what it means to *be* the body of Christ. We enter the drama of God living in us.

In contemplation, worshipers become a "living sacrifice." We become a temple, a space marked out for God. We become a template, a pattern that forms an accurate copy of God's shape. God becomes fixed in our memory, in our action, and in our character. We begin to live out our lives sacramentally. Individually and communally, we become Jesus' hands, eyes, feet, and heart. We gain mystical union in God's acting self, the body of Christ. True believers, individually and corporately, become the *face* in which people can recognize God, the *place* where they can find God, and the *space* where people can experience God without crowding him out or making him too small.

Ultimately, spiritual reading is spiritual living. It is the ongoing reality of "Christ in [us], the hope of glory" (Col. 1:27).

LECTIO DIVINA AS A GROUP PROCESS

The six sessions in this book have been designed both for individual study and for use in a small group setting. Of course, the discipline of *lectio divina* is not something a minister, a Bible teacher, or a small group can do *for* you. No one can be a disciple of Christ on your behalf. Dietrich Bonhoeffer wrote in *Life Together,* "Let him who cannot be alone beware of community" (p. 77). Spiritually empty Christians who depend exclusively on the small group process for their growth usually end up feeling just as empty and unfulfilled as when they first joined the group. However, when participants in the group share the energy and truth they derive from the discipline of their time alone with God, then the small group becomes an important transforming community.

So Bonhoeffer added, "Let him who is not in community beware of being alone." While *lectio divina* is an individual discipline, others are involved along the way. These others are

- the writers of the Bible who pray with us and who teach us God's Word.
- fellow believers who have left us a rich legacy of inspirational prayers and models of holy living.
- Bible scholars who provide commentaries and other aids for studying God's written Word.
- pastors, mentors, elders, and spiritual directors who guide us through our disciplines and hold us accountable.
- a church of fellow believers who admonish us when we're idle, encourage us when we're fainthearted, help us when we're weak, and show patience with our faltering attempts at serious discipleship.

Our fellow small group members can also be important motivators to help us learn and grow from this discipline. The goal of this six-session introduction to *lectio divina* is to enable you to work together in a small group setting so that you can encourage each other and hold each other accountable as you learn an important means of spiritual formation.

In order to accomplish this goal, your group will need a high level of commitment to the goal and to each other. Participants will need to know and trust each other. They will need to devote at least an hour to this material at group meetings, and work through it on their own between meeting times. They will need a place to meet in a quiet and peaceful setting that lends itself to meditation and reflection. Finally, the group will also require a leader who will carefully prepare for each session, deciding where and how to use the suggestions for leaders found in the margins of this book.

Although we hope that you will use *lectio divina* as outlined here, if you decide not to follow all of its steps you'll still be able to use this material as a meaningful study of John 17. In this intensely powerful Scripture passage, we hear the prayer that Jesus prays for us, his followers, before his crucifixion. However you use *At One with Jesus,* we pray that your reading and reflection on the prayer of our great High Priest will lead you into an odyssey of spiritual formation, a journey of faith in which you will become more at one with our risen and ascended Savior and Lord.

ONE

Glorify Yourself in Me

John 17:1-5, 10, 22

READING

Becoming Familiar with the Passage

1. Read John 17. Enter the written Word of God.

    This chapter is commonly referred to as the intercessory, or high priestly, prayer of Christ. It contains the last words of substance that the disciples hear from Jesus before his crucifixion. The words are spoken by Jesus to his Father, but Jesus also intends his disciples to hear them.

    This prayer lets you look deeply into the heart of Jesus. It admits you into the inner temple of holy desire; it is sacred ground; it is a burning bush of pure light. As you approach it, recognize that you're on holy ground. Begin to quiet your mind and tongue. Listen reverently and submissively.

    The prayer of Christ is spoken in the shadow of the cross. It is truly an appropriate prayer to learn as you begin your spiritual journey toward the cross of Good Friday and the open tomb of Easter.

> **Leader: Welcome the participants and spend time getting to know each other. Sing a few songs if the group is comfortable with that. When you're ready to begin, offer a prayer and ask one or more volunteers to read John 17 aloud. Then ask participants to read the introductory comments on their own.**

Seeking the Spirit's Light

1. Before re-reading God's Word, enter a time of silence. During this time, "breathe in" the Holy Spirit. Become aware first of your actual breathing. Settle down. Be quieted. Center your thoughts in your heart. Imagine, as you breathe in deeply, that you are inhaling the Holy Spirit. As you breathe out fully, imagine that you are exhaling your own sinful spirit. You don't need to formulate sentences in your mind right now. Just imagine the spiritual process accompanying your physical breathing.

> **Leader: Quietly explain how you will lead the group in this next section.**

2. Silently, in your mind, begin to say to God each of the following:

(as you inhale)	*(as you exhale)*
Lord Jesus Christ	have mercy on me
Jesus increase	self decrease
Spirit of God	spirit of self
praise you, Lord!	forgive me, Lord!

> **Leader: Offer a brief audible prayer for illumination on behalf of the group, asking the Spirit to speak through the written Word of God. Then invite participants to re-read the passage suggested.**

the mind of the Spirit	the lust of the flesh
the glory of God	the pride of life
Triune God	(your full name)

3. Re-read John 17:1-5, 10, 22 to yourself quietly and slowly.

Seeking Understanding

Leader: Ask participants to take approximately ten minutes to read the following reflections for themselves, or to take turns reading each paragraph aloud.

1. When studying these verses on your own, you can employ the inductive and deductive methods, using resources like those mentioned in the introduction to gain insight into the text. To facilitate group study, here are some thoughts that came out of my own reading of and meditation on these verses. Individual readers may find them helpful as well.

   Verses 1-5 are Christ's specific prayer for himself. He asks two things from his Father. The first is "Father . . . Glorify your Son, that your Son may glorify you" (v. 1). By linking this request for glory with the statement "Father, the time has come," Jesus shows that he is praying for his crucifixion. In chapter 12 of John, the linkage between *glory* and *cross* was clearly established:

   > Jesus answered them, "The hour has come for the Son of Man to be glorified. Very truly, I tell you, unless a grain of wheat falls into the earth and dies, it remains just a single grain; but if it dies, it bears much fruit. Those who love their life lose it, and those who hate their life in this world will keep it for eternal life."
   > —John 12:23-25, NRSV

   We find Jesus' second request in John 17:5: "And now, Father, glorify me in your presence with the glory I had with you before the world began." Here Jesus asks that his divinity may be seen after his humanity has been proven. He asks that his cross may lead to resurrection glory. He asks that God will be revealed through his return to the Father (see Phil. 2:5-11).

   In verses 10 and 22, Christ says that he is glorified in his disciples because he passed on to them the glory he received from the Father. This might lead each of us to the following chain of thought:

   - I am a disciple of Christ.
   - As a disciple I am called by Christ to live to the glory of God.

- The way I live to God's glory is by receiving from Christ the glory he received from the Father and reflecting it in my life.
- I need to learn what the glory of God is and how Christ showed it if I am to live to the glory of God in the truest sense of the word.

From Scripture we learn

- that the Hebrew word for *glory* literally means *weight* or *substance*. This lent itself to the idea that people who possess glory (people of substance) are laden with riches, power, and position. For God's people, however, real glory is not heavy with those things; it consists of the goodness and holiness we reflect from God.
- that the revelation of God's glory was sometimes like a devouring fire or like a brightly shining light. This light was closely linked with the shining of God's loving, forgiving, merciful character.
- that Christ is the one who most fully reveals and reflects the glory of God. He was sent to earth to show the true character of God in all his goodness, holiness, love, and justice. Jesus reflects the glory of God in a personal and direct way: "The Word became flesh and made his dwelling among us. We have seen his glory, the glory of the One and Only, who came from the Father, full of grace and truth" (John 1:14).
- that the blessing of God's glory in believers is described by Paul as "Christ in you" (Col. 1:27).
- that believers will share in Christ's glory when their bodies are raised, and they will appear with Christ in glory at his second coming.

The unique emphasis that the gospel of John contributes is that Christ's sufferings are revealed as his glorification. This fact holds several implications for our lives:

- God's limitless love came to its fullest, most brilliant expression on the cross of Christ: "For God so loved the world that he gave his one and only Son . . ." (John 3:16).
- The best way to bring glory to God is to obey him perfectly. On the cross, Christ's obedience to God reached its peak.
- The cross is the gateway to glory. Without the cross, Christ would have no crown; without humiliation, Christ would have had no exaltation; without service,

> **Leader:** Ask participants to move on to exercise 2. Ask each of them to tell which verse they chose, and why. Then take another ten minutes to share any insights or inspiration received from the reading and study up to this point.

> **Leader:** Ask your group to take approximately five minutes to work through exercises 1 and 2.

> **Leader:** After allowing time for exercise 2, ask if any participants are willing to share with the group what they received from the Spirit of God through their meditation. Did they hear God? What did God say to them? Don't push for responses, and feel free to share your own reflections with the group.

Christ would have no reward. For Jesus, the cross represented the beginning of the way back to God.

- My body is the temple of God the Spirit, in which I am called to glorify God (1 Cor. 6:19-20). The glory God gave to Christ has been given to me too (John 17:22). What glorifies God is not my money, my power, or my position; God is glorified when my life reflects Christ's glory, his obedience, his love, and his willingness to bear the cross of humble service and sacrifice for others. Am I willing to live in this way to the glory of God?

2. Read John 17:1-5, 10, 22 once again. Select one verse to memorize this coming week.

MEDITATION

1. As you take the second step in the spiritual discipline of *lectio divina*, pray silently the four meditation phrases below. Repeat each phrase several times before the face of God. Let the repitition flow with your breathing.

> Glorify yourself in me, Lord Christ.
> Father, the time of glory for me has come.
> Lord Jesus Christ, help me live to your glory.
> Glory be to God—Father, Son, and
>   Holy Spirit.

2. With these phrases echoing in your soul, select one of them and bring it forward in your consciousness. Meditate on it. Use this phrase as an exercise tool for your mind. Let it percolate in your thoughts. In Paul's terms, set your mind on the Spirit. Mix the ingredients of the verses we have looked at in John 17 with this phrase, with thoughts of your life, with experiences and dreams, with all you have seen, heard, and sensed. In the words of Bonhoeffer, "Go into the unfathomable depths of a particular sentence and word. . . . Expose [yourself] to the specific word until it addresses [you] personally" (*Life Together*). Wait upon the Holy Spirit to bring the Word home to your heart, to enlighten you so that you can actually experience what it is to "hear" God. This "hearing" God is the other, the answering, side of prayer.

PRAYER

1. Now you are ready to enter the prayer *(oratio)* phase of the *lectio divina* discipline. Begin by spending about five minutes in spontaneous prayer. Let your prayers reflect the inspiration of the Scripture passage as much as possible. Let your prayers be confessional and thankful. Later on, other

kinds of spontaneous prayer will be suggested (such as aspiration, adoration, offering, praise, petition, and intercession).

2. Read the following prayer aloud:

"Called to Glory"

When I ask you, Lord Christ, to glorify
   yourself in me
as the Father glorified himself in you,
I sense I am requesting an awesome thing.
Your glory was heavy, not easy to carry.
So it causes me to tremble
to think of living my life to the glory of God.
It's definitely more than an empty religious
   cliché.

When the hour of glory came for you,
   O Christ,
it was the moment of your cross.
It was an eternity of God-forsakenness
compacted into those excruciating moments of crucifixion.
It was an immense heaviness of passion so
   dramatic and real
that it cast a light over the whole world.
It was blood so real, flesh so open,
that the dye of your love colored all the
   earth.
It was your unmitigated suffering out of
   which flowed
the glory of your unspeakable love.

If the hour has truly come for me, my Lord,
to receive the glory first given you,
then I am most afraid,
but humbly challenged as well.
Can I possibly cast off the weights, the
   glories
of my wisdom, my might, my riches,
and boast only in this:
that I understand and know you, the Lord,
who practices steadfast love, justice, and
   righteousness in the earth?
For in these things is your heart delighted!
These, truly, are the things substantial,
the weights of glory which can make my
   life count.

Leader: Lead your group in a time of spontaneous prayer as suggested in exercise 1. Ask one person to conclude these prayers. Then read the prayer in exercise 2 together as an expression of communal worship. Read in unison or have participants take turns.

But am I up to the call?
I don't want to die!
I have so much for self I want to satisfy,
so much in self I want to fulfill,
so much by self I want to do.

Jesus, if I am to shoulder the weight of glory
borne by you and extended to me,
I must be mightily visited by your Spirit.
I must be emboldened, enlightened,
    empowered
beyond the frail limits of my human gifts.
Come to me, Lord. Come to me.

I want to sense your loving presence so
    passionately
that nothing else can distract me from the
    way of the cross.
Glorify yourself in me, Jesus.
In myself I am powerless to live to your
    glory.
Only you can do so through me.

"Grant to me your sacred presence;
then my faith will ne'er decline.
Comfort me and help me onward;
fill with love this heart of mine.

"Dwell in me, O blessed Spirit,
gracious Teacher, Friend divine!
For the kingdom work that calls me,
O prepare this heart of mine."
    (Text Martha J. Lankton, 1929, alt.)
Amen.

3. Take a moment for silent reflection. Ask the Holy Spirit to make this prayer truly yours.

CONTEMPLATION

This part of the *lectio divina* discipline cannot be done in the group. This must be done after you go home—into your family, into your church, into your neighborhood, into your occupation, into your world. This is the point at which you become an intentional contemplative, a Christian disciple resolved to become the Word lived. Contemplation is practiced as you continue to set your mind on the Spirit, to hold fast the Word of life, to pray the Scriptures you internalize, to practice the presence of Christ incessantly.

Leader: Review the Contemplation section with your group. Ask group members how you can make subsequent sessions more meaningful to them. If there is consensus on any of the suggestions, adjust subsequent sessions accordingly. Agree on the time and place of the next meeting, and close the session with a song or a brief spoken prayer.

Here are a few suggestions for the week to come:
- Read John 17:1-5, 10, 22 each day. As time allows, follow the first three steps of the discipline throughout the week at your own pace.
- Work on the verse you've agreed to memorize. Let it enter your thoughts often. *Pray* the Scriptures you've internalized in this way. Put the verse on a card and carry it with you for memory reference throughout the week. Remember, the key to memorization is repetition. Say the verse over and over until it becomes synonymous with breathing. Let it become a natural part of you, written on your heart. Let the memorized Word on which you set your mind become a subliminal message from the Spirit. As Paul encourages, "Be joyful always; pray continually; give thanks in all circumstances . . ." (1 Thess. 5:16-18).
- Share with a friend or someone in your family what you are learning through your *lectio divina* reading of John 17.
- Read "Called to Glory," the prayer used earlier in this session, for one of your personal or family devotion times.
- Consider developing a journal of prayers you write and/or collect from other believers.
- Live your faith. Let the Word read, meditated on, and prayed over become an incarnate Word—a Word embodied in your living! A true contemplative is not necessarily someone who lives in a hermitage, a monastery, or a convent. He or she is someone in whom the Word of God is acted out, in whom the glory of God is manifested in the flesh. All the glory of self fades away when the light of Christ's glory begins to shine through.
- Rest in Christ. The action of the contemplative's life is always and only the action of Christ. It is the action produced by resting in Christ. It is the doing produced by being ready, for once, not to do things. It is the increase of Christ and the decrease of self.

TWO

Finish Your Work in Me

John 17:4, 6-8

READING

1. Read John 17. Enter the written Word of God.
2. Pray for illumination by saying:

   > O God, you are my God.
   > I seek you.
   > My soul thirsts for you.
   > My flesh faints for you,
   > as in a dry and weary land where no water is.
   >
   > Lead me, Lord, today
   > through study, meditation, and prayer.
   > Lead me from information to inspiration,
   > from inspiration to communion,
   > from communion to incarnation.
   > Lead me, Lord, finally,
   > to the realization and materialization of
   >   yourself in me.
   > Transform me, Lord, by the renewal of my
   >   mind.
   > Lead me, Lord, to yourself
   > in all my thoughts, emotions, and intentions.
   > Amen.

3. Read John 17:4, 6-8 again, quietly and slowly.
4. Study the passage. Again, I've provided notes based on my reading and meditation. Take a few minutes now to read the following reflections:

   Though Jesus died a violent death as a young man, as he approached the end of his life he prayed, "I have brought you glory on earth by completing the work you gave me to do" (John 17:4).

   That's amazing—to come to the end of one's life and to be able to say "I've finished everything important. I've done all that God wanted." This is precisely what Jesus was able to say! Ironically, what enabled Jesus to finish the work of God was his capacity to *wait* on God.

   Of course, in just a few years of public ministry focused primarily in the minuscule land of Palestine, Jesus did not

> **Leader:** Welcome the participants. Get acquainted with any new group members. Spend a few minutes singing, if you wish. Lead a brief prayer. Then ask one or more people to read the passage aloud. Invite the group to read exercise 2 aloud together; then have them do exercise 3 on their own.

> **Leader:** Ask participants to take approximately five minutes to read the following reflections for themselves, or ask them to take turns reading each paragraph aloud.

heal all the sick; he did not raise all the dead; he did not seek out all the lost. As busy as Jesus was, with great crowds massing around him, he touched only a fraction of the need in Palestine, not to mention in all the rest of the hurting world. So how could he say "I've completed the work"?

He *didn't* say that. He said, to be precise, "I have brought you glory on earth by completing *the work you gave me to do.*" Jesus did all that the Father asked. He did what God called him to do—the important work—and left undone much of the work that urgently called for his attention.

But as we put Jesus' life into a more complete perspective, we can see that his obedience in sacrificing himself on the cross was sufficient to meet every urgent need of every person who calls on him.

Maybe that's why Jesus, though he worked hard, was never feverish, never frenzied, never tyrannized by the urgent. When Jesus' unbelieving half-brothers urged him to go to Jerusalem and show himself to the world at the Feast of Tabernacles, Jesus responded by saying, "The right time for me has not yet come; for you any time is right" (7:6). When several Pharisees came to Jesus and urged him to leave Jerusalem because of Herod's threat to kill him, Jesus answered them, "Go tell that fox, 'I will drive out demons and heal people today and tomorrow, and on the third day I will reach my goal.' In any case, I must keep going today and tomorrow and the next day—for surely no prophet can die outside Jerusalem!" (Luke 13:32-33). John reports in his gospel that when Jesus heard that his friend Lazarus was ill, "he stayed where he was two more days" (John 11:6).

In his book *The Discipline and Culture of the Spiritual Life*, A. E. Whitehead says of Jesus:

> Here in this Man is adequate purpose . . . inward rest, that gives an air of leisure to His crowded life; above all there is in this Man a secret and a power of dealing with the waste-products of life, the waste of pain, disappointment, enmity, death—turning to divine uses the abuses of man, transforming arid places of pain to fruitfulness, triumphing at last in death, and making a short life of thirty years or so, abruptly cut off, to be a 'finished' life. We cannot admire the poise and beauty of this human life, and then ignore the things that made it.
>
> —As quoted by Charles Hummel in
> *The Tyranny of the Urgent*, p. 7

The secret of Jesus' work is found in Mark 1:35: "Very early in the morning, while it was still dark, Jesus got up, left the house and went off to a solitary place, where he prayed." As Charles Hummel wrote about Jesus' prayerful life in his booklet *The Tyranny of the Urgent,* "Here is the secret of Jesus' life and work for God: He prayerfully waited for His Father's instructions and for the strength to follow them. Jesus had no divinely-drawn blueprint; He discerned the Father's will day by day in a life of prayer. By this means He warded off the urgent and accomplished the important" (p. 8).

MEDITATION

Today in meditation you will go beyond observation of Christ's finished life to evaluation of your own ongoing, *un*finished life. You can do this by reflecting on three quotations.

1. Read the following quotation by Paul Marshall:

   Leader: Ask someone to read this passage aloud.

   > For decades we have awaited the arrival of the leisure society. Futurologists have long dreamed of a world with little work to do. . . . Instead, we work longer and longer. . . . The average American's paid work week is three hours longer than it was 20 years ago. Our 'labor-saving' devices may make some tasks easier, but as a result, we simply do more things and work longer to pay for those devices. Faxes and cellular phones don't free us from the workplace, they simply extend the workplace to anywhere we go. . . . We are harried and hassled, living like gerbils in their wheels, dashing madly and getting nowhere. . . .
   >
   > Are Christians different? Yes. We are often worse. We have jobs and families like everyone else. But we also have the church. . . . We rest less than God does. . . . We also work to justify ourselves. Despite our claims of justification by faith, we tend to feel that our worth is shown in our exertion.
   >
   > —Paul Marshall, "Living Like Gerbils," *Christianity Today,* April 27, 1992

2. Let the main idea sink in. Be quiet for a few moments before you respond to it.

3. Now evaluate the quotation. How do you see it applying to you? To your church(es)?

Leader: Give participants a few minutes to reflect on the quotation, then ask them to discuss the questions in exercise 3. Invite a volunteer to read the next quotation from Charles Hummel and the comments related to it in exercise 4.

4. Charles Hummel relates how he was once told by an experienced cotton mill manager "Your greatest danger is letting the urgent things crowd out the important" (*The Tyranny of the Urgent*, p. 4). How true this is! The telephone rings, you run off to meet its imperious demand, but deep inside you remember the untouched Bible, the unspoken prayers, the unanswered letters, the promised but never-carried-out fun times with the kids, the needed but never-made visits, the creative projects that gather dust, the neglected private place of quiet.

Leader: Ask participants to think about Hummel's observations for a while. Then ask each person to share with the group their response to exercise 6. After the discussion, have a volunteer read the next quote.

5. Again, be still for a moment and reflect prayerfully on what was just read.

6. Identify something important in your life that is being put on hold because of the priority you give to the urgent. Be honest, humble, and transparent.

7. Read the following quotation by Kosuke Koyoma, a Japanese theologian:

> God walks 'slowly' because he is love. If he is not love he would have gone faster. Love has its speed. It is an inner speed. . . . It is a different kind of speed from the technological speed to which we are accustomed. . . . It goes on in the depth of our life . . . at three miles an hour. It is the speed we walk and therefore it is the speed the love of God walks.
>
> —*Three Mile an Hour God*, p. 7

Leader: Ask your group to do exercise 8, then lead them in a brief discussion of exercise 9.

8. Meditate prayerfully. Wait on God to receive the full impact from Koyoma's words.

9. What is the secret to keeping pace with God—to walking at that "slow pace of love"?

PRAYER

Leader: Invite the group to enter into a time of prayer as suggested in exercise 1. Tell participants that they may pray silently, or, if they wish, offer brief sentence prayers aloud. Tell them that you will lead them in the prayer suggested in exercise 2. You'll read the first part in unison, then take turns reading the second part before closing the prayer together.

1. Offer prayers of confession. Confess your sins to God that you may be healed. Ask God to slow you down, to show you what is important, and to deliver you from the tyranny of the urgent.

2. Read, as an expression of worship, the following prayer based on John 17:4, 6-8:

"God's Work Accomplished"

Read in unison:

O persevering and perfect Christ,
how half-hearted and flawed my work
    appears,
even when added up over several decades,
as compared to the accomplishment of your
    work
which the Father gave you to finish in but a
    few years.

I could live to be a hundred, even a
    thousand years
and would not yet be able to testify:
"I have brought you glory on earth
by completing the work you gave me to do."
Rarely have I ever finished anything.
My work, though often well-intended,
and done at great expense of time and
    energy,
is such a pitiful sum of good when added up
and set next to your own.

Take turns reading the following paragraphs:

You have finished your work in glorifying the Father. I have left kingdom work undone by glorifying self.

You have finished your work in giving eternal life to all whom God gave you. I have left such work to others.

You have finished your work in manifesting the Father's name. I have busied myself with advancing the acclaim given my own name.

You have finished your work in passing on to your disciples the words of God. I have passed on little more than my own words of wisdom.

You have finished your work in leaving behind a small core of committed disciples. I have worried too much over church growth and fretted over membership numbers.

You have finished your work in showing your followers the love to make them one. I have alienated my brothers and sisters with truth too harshly spoken.

You have finished your work in a love of total self-giving. I have inhibited God's work with my selfishness and self-service.

You have finished your work in keeping and guarding your own. I have too often pleased myself, and put the unity of the church at risk.

You have finished your work in passing on the joy of God's presence. I have not steadfastly endured the cross for the joy set before me.

You have finished your work of modeling how to be *in* but not *of* the world. Sometimes I'm more *of* the world and less *in* it.

You have finished your work of demonstrating God's love for the whole world. My vision is limited, Lord, by its ethnicity and by my satisfaction with my privileged position.

Read in unison:

How can I get on with the task you have assigned me, Lord,
unless I stop doing my own thing and start doing yours?
Yet, even this isn't how to put the question and express the remedy.
I can't start doing your work any more than I can finish my own.
I need you, Spirit of Christ, to fill me anew to overflowing.
You must do in me what I cannot start or finish.
I can do all things only through Christ who strengthens me!
But then the work is really yours, not mine.
Then all the glory goes to you, Father, as it should.
Then there is hope that your work in me will be accomplished.
Then I do not need years and years to attain my goals.

> It is enough to live each day in your strength
> and to your glory.
>
> Come, Holy Spirit, with all your quickening
> powers. Amen.

3. Take a moment for silent reflection. Ask the Holy Spirit to help you apply this prayer to your life.

CONTEMPLATION

1. Each day of the coming week, memorize and pray repeatedly this adaptation of John 17:4:

(as you inhale)	*(as you exhale)*
Lord Jesus Christ,	have mercy on me.
Lord Jesus Christ,	have mercy on me.
Lord Jesus Christ,	grant me your peace.
Lord Jesus Christ,	glorify yourself in me.
Lord Jesus Christ,	show me what is important.
Lord Jesus Christ,	finish your work in me.

   Take breathing pauses, little sabbaths, or time-outs during the day to utter this prayer. Catch your breath. Consider your strategy. Wait for directions. Let the Spirit show you the truth about God, about yourself, and about your tasks. Remember in your prayer to center your thoughts on the triune God in your heart. God is there, at home, always ready to greet you with the salutation of grace.

2. Share the prayer "God's Work Accomplished" with your family or with a friend.

3. If you keep a prayer journal, write some brief prayers of confession. Focus on your sins of "drivenness," haste, and wasted opportunities to do God's will.

4. Remind yourself that if you live each moment for God—waiting upon God, loving God above all, seeking to understand and do God's will—then each moment will be fulfilled (made full) and life will receive its meaning. The push, the rush, will be over. You can relax and concentrate on giving yourself to God and to others. You don't have to do this or that before you die. You only have to do each moment what God shows you to do.

5. "Be joyful always; pray continually; give thanks in all circumstances, for this is God's will for you in Christ Jesus" (1 Thess. 5:16-18).

Leader: Ask the group to read the prayer once more and to reflect on it for a few moments. Ask members how they did in practicing the contemplation exercises last week. Then urge them to complete the exercises listed here for next week. Close the session with some appropriate songs if you wish. Then offer a brief closing prayer.

Pray for Me
John 17:9

READING

1. Read John 17. Enter the written Word of God.
2. Pray for illumination by reciting the following prayer:

> Gracious and loving God, you know the deep inner patterns of my life that keep me from being totally yours. You know the misformed structures of my being that hold me in bondage to something less than your high purpose for my life. You also know my reluctance to let you have your way with me in these areas. Hear the deeper cry of my heart for wholeness and by your grace enable me to be open to your transforming presence in this reading. Lord, have mercy.
> —M. Robert Mulholland, Jr.,
> *Invitation to a Journey*, p. 19

3. Each person read, silently and slowly, John 17:9: "I pray for them. I am not praying for the world, but for those you have given me, for they are yours."
4. Read the following study notes.

Some of the last words of substance Jesus spoke to his disciples before he died were words of intercessory prayer. Words of parting are important words. They originate in the heart; they reflect our deepest concerns when everything else is being stripped away.

John 17 allows us to take a look deep into the heart of Jesus, to enter the inner sanctum of Christ's holy desire. Christ can be seen looking up to heaven, addressing the Father and praying for himself, then for his own, then for those whom his disciples will reach, and finally for the world held in God's loving heart.

Christ's prayer has immense scope. Yet it also has very personal focus. For example, in verses 11-19 Jesus makes these specific petitions for his disciples:

- "Holy Father, protect them by the power of your name—the name you gave me" (v. 11).

Leader: Welcome the participants. If you wish, join in some communal singing. Lead a brief prayer. Ask one or more people to read the passage aloud. Invite the group to recite together the prayer for illumination, then have them do exercise 3 on their own.

Leader: Ask participants to take approximately five minutes to read the following reflections for themselves, or ask them to take turns reading each paragraph aloud.

- "... so that they may be one as we are one" (v. 11).
- "... so that they may have the full measure of my joy within them" (v. 13).
- "My prayer is not that you take them out of the world but that you protect them from the evil one" (v. 15).
- "Sanctify them by the truth; your word is truth" (v. 17).

In verses 11-19, Jesus prays that *Christ*ians (bearers of Christ's name) will be protected in the world, that they will be held together in Trinity-like fellowship, that they will become completely joyful in Christ, and that they will become progressively holy through the internalized Word of God.

Leader: Ask your group to pray silently for a moment, then conclude with a brief spoken prayer. Ask a volunteer to read exercise 1 of the meditation section.

5. Pause for a moment of silent prayer in which you ask Jesus to pray for you.

MEDITATION

1. Read the following:

    It is quite common for us as believers to pray to Jesus. If we do not always pray directly *to* Jesus, then at least we pray *through* Jesus, approaching God in Jesus' name. It's less common for us to see ourselves as being prayed for *by* Jesus. Perhaps this thought of Christ's intercessory role is tucked deep into our subconscious mind as we pray. But seldom, if ever, do we find ourselves asking, "Jesus, pray for me." We're rarely quiet enough to let Jesus pray for us. We might ask, Why would Jesus have to pray for me? Doesn't he expect me to pray for myself and for others just like he prayed for himself and for others?

Leader: After asking the group to reflect on exercise 2, ask participants to take turns reading the suggested reasons provided in exercise 3, and ask all participants to read for themselves the meditative responses that follow each suggestion.

2. What reasons can you think of for asking Christ to pray for you?

3. Read the following suggested reasons for seeking Christ's continued intercession. After each reason there is a suggested meditative response.

    a. Awkward Hunters

    We need Jesus to pray for us because he is our guide in our pursuit of God. The God we know, who lives in our hearts, is still the God we seek: "O God, you are my God, earnestly I seek you" (Ps. 63:1). The pursuit of God is not a frenzied chase. God is not found by a spiritual hunter with a blabbering, noisy mouth. The pursuit of God is retreat from haste, from noise, from incessant talk. In a very real sense, to be in pursuit of God is to become a refugee—a refugee from perceived failure, from perceived success, and from a driven self. We ask our voices of self-defeat, self-pride, and self-control to be still. Our soul waits in silence. And in the stillness we whisper: Jesus, pray for me. Pioneer of faith, show me the way to God. Pray me into the presence of the Father, that I may become spiritually attuned enough to hear his voice out of the stillness, telling me:

> Be still and know that I am God;
> I'm right here by your side.
> Be still and know that I am God,
> and in my love abide.
> So few of you stop to hear the birds,
> stop to smell the fragrance in the air.
> My kingdom is within you;
> be still and find me there.
> —Evie, "Be Still," *Unfailing Love* (album);
> words and music by Tipi Charles

Response: Imagine yourself as a hunter in pursuit of God and then pray silently the following:

O God, you are my God; I seek you. But I'm not very good at it.

My search for you, Lord, is like that of a first-time hunter, chasing noisily through the woods, missing every sign of your presence, and causing such a racket that the animals can hardly keep from laughing at my performance. I sense they are laughing right under my nose. It is I who end up the prey to whatever beast might pounce on me.

It is no small relief, Lord, to know you are not laughing—you're amused, perhaps, but not laughing. It will take time for me to learn how to seek you, to find a quiet, worshipful spot and sit there, listening and observing until I have you in my sights.

Teach me, Lord, how to pray. Teach me the patience of unanswered prayer. "Speak, Lord, in the stillness, while I wait on thee; hush my heart to listen in expectancy" ("Speak, Lord, in the Stillness," *Hymns II*, InterVarsity, p. 140). Amen.

b. Jesus Knows When We Don't

Jesus must pray for us because he has perfect knowledge of God's will and of what is best for us. It can become very tiring and tedious to figure out what God needs to do for us and then express it adequately in prayer. After a while we begin to feel like we're heaping up empty phrases to the God who already *knows* what we need. Our prayer well soon runs dry. Sometimes we need to rest in the Lord.

Response: Pray silently: Bless me, Lord; have mercy on me, Lord; your will be done, Lord; pray for me, Jesus.

c. Christ's Voice in Us

We ask Jesus to pray for us because he has promised to convince our hearts of sin, righteousness, and judgment, through the Spirit of truth (John 16:8-15). This inner conviction, produced by the Spirit of Christ, becomes Christ's voice of prayer inside us.

Response: Pray silently now, and meditate on the meaning and application of the following:

> Jesus, pray for me.
> O Blessed Spirit of Truth,
> convince my heart of sin;
> convince my heart of righteousness;
> convince my heart of judgment. Amen.

d. When We Cannot Pray

We need Jesus to pray for us because sometimes we simply cannot pray. Like the psalmist in Psalm 77, we think of God in our wearied spirits and all we can do is moan. We meditate and our spirit faints. We are so troubled we cannot speak. All we can do is cry out for Christ's intercession, and the Holy Spirit "intercedes for us with groans that words cannot express" (Rom. 8:26).

Response: Breathe deeply several times. Each time you exhale, imagine that you are draining out your frustrations, fears, and sorrows. You are, as it were, sighing with feelings too deep for words. But then imagine that what you have exhaled has been blown into the heart of Christ. Imagine that he has taken your sighs and turned them into words that he is praying to the Father. Rest in God's peace.

e. Christ Is Our High Priest

We must continue to ask Christ to pray for us because, in the words of Hebrews 3:14, "we have come to share in Christ if we hold firmly till the end the confidence we had at first." Hebrews 9:24-26 specifies what that confidence is:

> For Christ did not enter a sanctuary made by
> human hands, a mere copy of the true one,
> but he entered into heaven itself, now to appear in the presence of God on our behalf.
> Nor was it to offer himself again and again,

as the high priest enters the Holy Place year after year with blood that is not his own; for then he would have had to suffer again and again since the foundation of the world. But as it is, he has appeared once for all at the end of the age to remove sin by the sacrifice of himself.
—Hebrews 9:24-26, NRSV

Response: Bow in silent meditation and picture the scene of Hebrews 9:24-26 quoted above. Affirm to God that Christ's sacrifice is your confidence.

f. We Belong to Christ

Christ's prayers for us are still necessary because we have been given to Jesus by God (John 17:6, 10, 12). Jesus gave himself to God. God gave us back to Jesus. We belong to Jesus. His prayers for us are part of his responsible stewardship on our behalf.

Response: Pray silently:

> Jesus, I belong to you.
> Thank you for taking such good care of me.
> Thank you for praying for me.
> Your prayers are an immense comfort.
> I love you, Lord! Amen.

g. He Knows Our Weakness

Christ is still an indispensable intercessor for us because he knows our infirmities better than anyone. The reason he became a human being was "in order that he might become a merciful and faithful high priest in service to God, and that he might make atonement for the sins of the people. Because he himself suffered when he was tempted, he is able to help those who are being tempted" (Heb. 2:17-18).

Response: Pray silently:

> Blessed Lord and Holy Spirit, stand by my
>   side with strength.
> You know my weaknesses.
> Do not let me be tested beyond my breaking
>   point.
> I know you understand.
> Have mercy on me.
> Pray for me. Amen.

h. Empowered Witness
Christ's prayers for you are still needed because his prayers give your witness to lost people effectual power (John 17:20-26).

Response: Pray:
Jesus, please remember in your intercessions
all those to whom I have witnessed,
all those to whom I am witnessing,
all those to whom I hope to bring a witness.
Amen.

Leader: Take time to discuss the participants' answers to this question. Be prepared to "break the ice" with your own response.

4. When do you sense most deeply the need for Jesus to pray for you?

PRAYER

1. Read the following:

One very good way to have Christ pray for us is to ask him to do so. Another is to borrow his words. In John 17:8, 14, Jesus tells the Father that he has given his disciples the words that he first received from the Father. These words are sanctifying because they are truth. Jesus calls his own to worship him in spirit and in truth (John 4:23).

Leader: Move your group into the discipline of prayer by reading these comments aloud to them, then inviting them to do exercise 2.

The borrowed words of God are the Scriptures. Praying the memorized words of Scripture is a wonderful way of turning your prayer over to Jesus' control. It brings such relief of heart not to have to carry the prayer burden alone. When our Bible-directed prayers follow quiet meditation on God's Word, then the words of Scripture themselves generate new insights into our true needs. We find the words of Scripture blossoming forth into spontaneous prayers. Though they are our own, they do not feel like our own. They feel like ecstatic utterances impelled by the Spirit. In these very surprising utterances we hear the voice of God speaking back. Then we know we are praying in the will of God. Such prayers surely do not become stale, frustrating, or tiresome. They have great power in their effects.

2. Each person, in silence, repeat John 17:9 at least three times to the Lord. Meditate on whatever strikes your heart in this verse. Then let the Spirit of Christ produce spontaneous utterances within your spirit. Listen to whatever the Spirit gives.

3. As an expression of your worship, read the following prayer based on John 17:9, pausing briefly for reflection after each verse:

Leader: Invite participants to join you in a communal reading of this prayer.

> "Pray for Me, Jesus"
>
> It is of immense comfort, Jesus,
> to know that you are praying for me.
> Since the Father has given me to you,
> I am yours and must be kept by your prayers.
>
> I do pray for myself—
> perhaps more than I should
> and often not enough for my neighbor—
> but sometimes my prayers falter.
> They are imperfectly spoken, selfishly
>   intended;
> they are diminished by subliminal unbelief,
>   by unconfessed sin;
> they are tormented by fears and anxieties;
> they can be perfunctory and trite.
> I can be demanding and controlling.
> My scope of vision can be so narrow, so
>   individualistic.
> My prayer search can be mere self-discovery
> rather than seeking after you with all my
>   heart.
>
> So praying for my self is not enough.
> Even when my prayers are sincere,
> even when they are driven by a spiritual
>   passion,
> still they need reinterpretation by you.
>
> I trust you, Lord Christ, I depend on you
> to make my prayers acceptable to God.
> As my prayers run through the filter of your
>   mind
> and reemerge from your mouth,
> they change from milky river water,
> produced by floods and running out of
>   control,
> into crystal-pure spring waters seeking out
>   the heart of God
> and drawing him to return to me as living
>   Spirit.
>
> I ask you, Lord Jesus Christ,
> to keep on praying for me.

Do not lose patience with my flaccid
    prayers.
Do not despair over my faltering speech, my
    petty vision.

Lord Jesus Christ,
have mercy on me.
Lord Jesus Christ,
have mercy on me.
Lord Jesus Christ,
grant me your peace.

I cannot rest, I cannot enjoy sabbath,
unless your Spirit assures me that I'm not
    praying alone.
I need an advocate, an ally, an interpreter,
    a mediator, a priest.
I need your prayers, Jesus.
Pray in me, pray through me, pray for me,
    pray in spite of me.
Blessed Jesus, do not ever, ever give up
    on me.
Preserve me and my faith in your priestly
    intercessions.
Remember me whenever your face is turned
    to the Father
to lay before him all those in this world
    whom he so loves,
and for whom he sent you to die.

Thank you, Jesus. Amen.

CONTEMPLATION

Leader: Once again, ask members of the group to share the thoughts, insights, frustrations, and blessings they received through their practice of contemplation since your last meeting. Allow time for mutual encouragement and accountability. Urge them to complete the exercises listed under this section. Close the session with singing and/or with prayer.

1. Remember that contemplation is the lifestyle of reading, meditation, and prayer. You have entered through your reading into the written Word of God, the world of God, and the personal Word of God. During the coming week you will enter the *work* of God, which is an extension of his rest. God's work is recreational and celebrative. It is relaxing and renewing because it is his work within you, not your work for him.

2. Each time you pray this week, take a moment to ask Jesus to pray for you, and tell him you trust him to do so.

3. Spend some quiet time this week repraying the eight response prayers in the "Meditation" part of Session Three.

4. Read "Pray for Me, Jesus" during personal and/or family devotion time.

5. Try recording on the tape of your mind the simple repetitive prayer that is sometimes called "The Jesus Prayer." It goes like this:

>   Lord Jesus Christ, have mercy on me.
>   Lord Jesus Christ, have mercy on me.
>   Lord Jesus Christ, grant me your peace.

Put your mental tape player in "replay" mode and let the tape of this prayer keep running as a subliminal message you are incessantly sending to God. You will be setting your mind on the Spirit, covering all that you do, think, and say with the name of Christ.

At first you will have to be somewhat intentional in your repetition, but eventually the prayer will become as regular as your breathing or heartbeat. You will feel the prayer as you go about your work. A spirit of rest will enter your work.

Sometimes deliberately vary "The Jesus Prayer" Substitute words like:

>   Lord Jesus Christ, pray for me still.
>   Lord Jesus Christ, show me the way.
>   Lord Jesus Christ, love me forever.
>   Blessed Holy Spirit, breathe on me anew.
>   Spirit of the living God, fall afresh on me.
>   God my Father, I wait for you.
>   Father in heaven, I worship you. Amen.

Keep Me and Guard Me
John 17:11-15

READING

1. Read John 17.

2. I meet you, Lord, at your home address: my body. I see you in your glory sitting on the throne of my heart. The light of your faithfulness, mercy, and wisdom emanates from your countenance. It puts a borrowed radiance on my face so that I am penitent but not ashamed. It puts an assurance of your grace in my soul. It makes me want to kneel in reverence before you.

   Wait upon God in silence; after a moment continue to read.

   All I can say is: Have mercy on me, Lord. I am unworthy of your love. I am a person of unclean lips, heart, and mind. I wait upon you to speak to me the words of life again. Your word is a lamp to my feet, a light to my path. Speak, Lord, for I am listening! Amen.

3. Read John 17:11-15 silently and slowly. Pause after each phrase, allowing the Spirit to illumine the meaning.

4. Lift up your hearts to heaven and pray this prayer out loud:

   > Our Father in heaven,
   > hallowed be your name.
   > Glorify yourself in us,
   > as you did in Jesus,
   > and as you do still through Christ.
   >
   > Let our study, meditation, and prayer today
   > be kept pure and holy.
   > Keep us in the Spirit.
   > Fulfill your joy in us.
   > Guard us from error and divisiveness
   > in our reception of the precious Word
   > that you have given to us.
   > And pray for us, Jesus, in this hour,
   > that we may be sanctified in truth and love.
   > Amen.

Leader: Welcome participants. If you wish, join in some communal singing. Ask someone to read the passage, then ask someone else to read aloud the prayer for illumination. Ask the reader to pause between paragraphs to allow participants a minute or two for silent prayer.

Leader: Invite participants to read this passage as suggested, then lead them in the prayer that follows.

Leader: Ask participants to take turns reading paragraphs of these notes to the group.

5. Read the following study notes.

   Two closely linked words provide the key to the study of verses 11-15. They are the words *keep* and *guard*. In verse 12, Jesus prays: "While I was with them I kept them in thy name which thou hast given me; I have guarded them . . ." (RSV).

   The best synonym for *keep* is *preserve*. It is often followed by the preposition *in:* I keep them in my name; I preserve them in my vision.

   The best synonym for *guard* is *protect*. It is often followed by the preposition *from:* I guard them from the world's hatred; I protect them from the evil one.

   Keep and *guard* are actually two sides of the same coin: to be *protected from* is to be *kept in*. Jesus interconnects these words in five different ways:

   a. "Protect them from the evil one," or "Keep them strong in the Holy Spirit." See John 14:16-17, 26; 15:26; 16:7-8, 13 for Jesus' promises regarding the entry of the Spirit into the lives of his disciples.

   b. "Protect them from vanity," or "Keep them in your name given to me." The point of being preserved in the name of Christ is to be kept in his power, purity, and integrity and to be protected from turning the name of God into a meaningless chant or making his name seem cheap by dishonoring it in a compromised (culture-driven) life and witness.

   c. "Protect them from fraction," or "Keep them in unity." Jesus prays that his disciples may be guarded from discord in the body of Christ by being held in the spiritual dynamic of oneness that exists between Father and Son: "so that they may be one as we are one" (v. 11). Jesus' prayer is a petition for unity, not for unanimity, uniformity, or union. In *John: The Gospel of Belief*, Merrill C. Tunney writes:

   > Unanimity means absolute concord of opinion within a given group of people. Uniformity is complete similarity of organization or of ritual. Union implies political affiliation without necessarily including individual agreement. Unity requires oneness of inner heart and essential purpose, through the possession of a common interest or a common life. . . . Jesus did not pray for absolute unanimity of mind, nor for uniformity of practice, nor for union of visible

organization, but for the underlying unity of spiritual nature and of devotion which would enable His people to bear a convincing testimony before the world (p. 248-249).

d. "Protect them from the world's hatred," or "Keep them in your Word"—the Word first given to Jesus, then given by him to his followers. The world hates believers because it cannot own them; it cannot control them with social pressures and physical threats. The world feels threatened by believers because the light of believers' holy lives can expose the darkness of the lives of those whose practices are evil (see John 3:19-21). When David prayed for protection from his enemies in Psalm 17, he prayed also that God would keep him as the apple of God's eye, hidden in the shadow of God's wings, captivated by the vision of God's righteous face, which was the first thing he saw upon waking (Ps. 17:8, 15).

e. "Protect them from sorrow," or "Keep them in my joy." Sorrow refers to the suffering of loss: "Do not let your hearts be troubled. . . . if I go and prepare a place for you, I will come back and take you to be with me . . ." (John 14:1, 3). The antidote for sorrow is to be kept in the complete joy of Christ: "I say these things . . . so that they may have the full measure of my joy within them" (17:13). We experience joy through the blessed all-sufficiency of Christ's presence in which we abide (John 15:4) and in which we are kept.

MEDITATION

1. Here are three meditation phrases from our passage. Meditate on each phrase silently for a few minutes.

   - "that they may have the full measure of my joy within them" (v. 13)
   - "protect them by the power of your name—the name you gave me" (v. 11)
   - "the world has hated them, for they are not of the world" (v. 14)

2. Imagine the following images of joy. Try to form a mental picture of each scene:
   - a birth
   - a wedding
   - a lost sinner returning home

Leader: Invite your group to take five minutes or so to silently work through exercises 1 and 2 on their own.

- the entire Congress or House of Commons falling to its knees in genuine repentance
- a saint completing the final journey to her heavenly Father's home

Now pray silently, "Complete your joy in me, dear Lord." Repeat the prayer at least three times.

Leader: Ask the group to briefly discuss the two questions in exercise 3. Then ask them to take five minutes or so to work through the rest of the Meditation section on their own.

3. What is "joy in the Lord"? What is "completed joy"? Evaluate your own personal joy quotient.

4. Picture Jesus' character of joy as a fruit of the Spirit in you. This joy grows and ripens as Christ increases in you. So receive the increase of Christ by this breathing prayer:

(as you inhale)	*(as you exhale)*
The joy of Jesus	my dreariness
The joy of Jesus	my weariness
The joy of Jesus	my heaviness
The joy of Jesus	my emptiness
Jesus increase	self decrease
Jesus increase	self decrease
Jesus increase	self decrease
Amen.	

5. Think about the second meditation phrase above, "protect them by the power of your name" (17:11). Consider how you are a *Christ*ian—a bearer of Christ's name. Examine yourself before the face of God, privately asking yourself these questions:

   O Christ, do I bear your name unabashedly?
   Do others know I bear your name?
   Do I bear your name with integrity?
   Do I consciously and prayerfully carry your
       name into my activities throughout the day?

6. Refer to the third meditation phrase cited above, "the world has hated them, for they are not of the world" (v. 14). Humbly and privately let Christ evaluate your degree of worldliness by asking yourself these three questions:

   Lord, what is my spiritual condition?
   Am I loved by the world because it controls me?
   Or am I hated by the world because it can't own me?

Leader: Invite your group to engage communally in the prayers as suggested, centering their prayers around how God keeps and guards us. Encourage, but do not push, participants to pray aloud using sentence prayers. Times of silence are fine. Ask them to pray their own prayers of confession, petition, intercession, and thanksgiving during that time. Conclude the prayer time by leading them in reading together the prayer provided in exercise 3.

PRAYER

1. Now engage in a time of prayer based on your honest answers to the hard questions you asked yourself in your meditation.

2. Continue your time of prayer by sharing petitions (for self) and intercessions (for others) that flow out of your reading and reflection upon Christ's requests to the Father to keep and guard Jesus' followers. Also express thanksgiving to God for ways in which he has kept and guarded you.

3. As an expression of your worship, read the following prayer based on John 17:11-15. Pause for a moment of silent meditation after each verse:

> "Standing Guard"
>
> Truly, I believe your promise, Lord Jesus Christ,
> that you have begun a good work in me,
> that you will perfect it to the day of salvation.
> I honestly believe that your love will not let me go.
> I honestly believe that nothing can separate me from your love—
> ". . . neither death nor life, neither angels nor demons,
> neither the present nor the future, nor any powers,
> neither height nor depth, nor anything else in all creation. . . ."
> I trust your power to guard me so that I won't be lost.
> Your peace stands guard over my heart and mind.
>
> Praise be to you, O Christ! I am justified by your grace.
> I stand secure in this grace to which you have given me access.
> I rejoice in my hope of sharing the glory of God.
> Lord, without these assurances, I would be in the pit of despair.
>
> I confess the problem of my wandering and wayward heart.
> I confess my temptation to use your promises as an excuse, justifying my backslidings.
> Sin seems to have such attractive side benefits—

or so it seems in the passion of the moment.
How easily I push aside the thought of your Spirit
and enjoy the side-affections of sin for a moment.
How easily I justify taking a short break from radical spirituality.
How easily I call a brief time-out in my pursuit of victory in Christ.
How surprisingly clever my mind is, when set on the flesh.
It can make the foulest sin smell like a rose.

Lord Jesus Christ,
have mercy on me.
Lord Jesus Christ,
have mercy on me.
Lord Jesus Christ,
grant me your peace.

"Oh, to grace how great a debtor
daily I'm constrained to be!
Let thy goodness, like a fetter,
bind my wandering heart to Thee:
prone to wander, Lord, I feel it,
prone to leave the God I love;
here's my heart, O take and seal it;
seal it for thy courts above."

I ask you, Jesus, to extend your promised guardianship.
Cover me in those moments of utmost weakness
when "the lust of the flesh, the lust of the eyes,
and the pride of life" gang up in full assault upon my fragile senses.

Keep me, Lord; keep me in your righteousness.
Keep me, Lord; keep me in your name, which you have given me. Amen.

CONTEMPLATION

1. This week, each time you enter into prayer, begin with the following:

> **Leader:** Ask members to share how their practice of contemplation is going. What do they find difficult? What benefits are they experiencing? What helps them and encourages them in pursuing this spiritual discipline? Allow some time for the group to share their experiences, then conclude the session with singing and/or a closing prayer. Encourage them to follow the exercises listed under this section.

(as you inhale)	*(as you exhale)*
Lord Jesus Christ,	keep me in your Spirit;
Lord Jesus Christ,	protect me from evil.
Lord Jesus Christ,	keep me in your name;
Lord Jesus Christ,	protect me from vanity.

Lord Jesus Christ, keep me in unity;
Lord Jesus Christ, protect me from fraction.

Lord Jesus Christ, keep me in your Word;
Lord Jesus Christ, protect me from hatred.
Lord Jesus Christ, keep me in your joy;
Lord Jesus Christ, protect me from sorrow.

Lord Jesus Christ, have mercy on me.
Lord Jesus Christ, have mercy on me.
Lord Jesus Christ, grant me your peace.
Amen.

2. Read "Standing Guard" for personal or family devotions or both.
3. Each day, memorize and reinforce with prayer and meditation the words of John 17:11 and 14.
4. In prayer picture Christ on the cross lifted up, drawing you into his protective presence. Hold this image in your heart throughout the week and praise God without ceasing.

Abide with Me—in the World
John 17:14-16, 18

READING

1. Read John 17.
2. Pray this prayer for illumination:

   Enter my heart, O Holy Spirit,
   come in blessed mercy and set me free.
   Throw open, O Lord, the locked doors of my
      mind;
   cleanse the chambers of my thought for thy
      dwelling:
   light there the fires of thine own holy bright-
      ness in new understandings of truth.
   O Holy Spirit, very God, whose presence is
      liberty,
   grant me the perfect freedom
   to be thy servant
   today, tomorrow, evermore.
   —Eric Milner-White, as quoted in
   The Oxford Book of Prayer, p. 149

3. Read John 17:14-16, 18 again, silently and very slowly.
4. Read the following study notes.

   In praying for his disciples, Jesus spoke of them as belonging *in* the world, but not *to* it. But what did Jesus mean by *the world* as we hear him speak of it in the gospel of John? On the one hand, *the world* refers to people cut off from God. It is a kingdom with its own autonomous rules and its own humanistic ends. This world hates anyone aligned with Christ and with the revelation, the Word of God (John 8:23; 15:19; 17:14). To the world, the disciples of Christ represent a competing order, a control threat. Jesus' followers have God-given values that expose the world's evil and infuriate the world (John 3:19-20).

   Because the world hates Christ, his followers are tempted to compromise, to go with the flow, or to disengage, to get out of the stream. It's easiest to become either thoroughly worldly or hopelessly quietistic.

Leader: Welcome the participants. If you wish, join in some communal singing. Ask someone to read the passage, then pray in unison the prayer for illumination.

Leader: Invite the group to do exercise 3 for themselves; then invite them to read aloud and in turn the paragraphs of exercise 4.

But in the gospel of John, Jesus also refers to the world as a cosmos of creatures, things, and people that God made, takes pride in, and jealously protects. It is a cosmos God so loved that he gave his only Son to die for its redemption (John 3:16-17). The world is the very real earth to which Christ descended and the very real humanity into which he entered through his incarnation (John 1:3, 9-10).

The world, taken in this second sense, is fantastically beautiful, generous, and enjoyable. Yet at the same time it's deeply mired in the travail of entropy and suffering. This dual reality once again tempts Jesus' followers either to immerse themselves in the world or to colonize behind the high walls of the church, keeping the world out and remaining untouched by its pain and suffering. Christians often cancel out their witness of holiness in the world through secularism, through materialism, and through their deification of nature, possessions, or people. Others cop out by isolating themselves within Christian organizations, addressing the world only with judgmental legalisms, not with redemptive co-suffering.

Leader: Lead your group in discussing the questions in exercise 5.

5. Investigate the text a bit more by thinking these questions through:

   a. How did Jesus explain the world's hatred for Christians? (See v. 14.)

   b. Does the world belong to God or to the evil one? (See v. 15.)

   c. What does Christ imply by saying of his disciples, "They are not of the world, even as I am not of it" (v. 16)?

   d. What does Christ mean by telling his Father, "As you sent me into the world, I have sent them into the world" (v. 18)?

MEDITATION

Leader: Invite participants to read the couplets aloud in turn, pausing briefly between each couplet to allow the words to sink in.

1. Pray aloud the following meditation couplets. Pause after each couplet for a moment of silent meditation.

> Lord Jesus Christ,
> keep me from the world
> without letting me escape it.

> Lord Jesus Christ,
> I do not belong to the world,
> but do I not owe myself to it?

> Lord Jesus Christ,
> I am not to be of the world,
> but am I not to be in it?

Lord Jesus Christ,
the world is God's enemy
for whom you died.

Lord Jesus Christ,
the world is principalities and powers,
and people needing rescue by you.

Lord Jesus Christ,
the world is a driven culture
to which I am driven by your freedom.

Lord Jesus Christ,
the world is too much with me,
yet who in the world am I with?

Lord Jesus Christ,
worldliness without you is a vice;
worldliness in you is a virtue.

Lord Jesus Christ,
the world knew you not,
yet the world was made by you.

Lord Jesus Christ,
the world has fallen,
yet you have descended into it.

Lord Jesus Christ,
the world has lifted you up,
yet from the cross you draw it back.

Lord Jesus Christ,
the world loved darkness,
but you answered with light.

Lord Jesus Christ,
the world loved itself,
yet God so loved the world.

Lord Jesus Christ,
the world's no company to keep,
yet in suffering you are its companion.

Lord Jesus Christ,
keep me from the world
while leading me straight to it.

Lord Jesus Christ,
have mercy on me.
Abide with me—in the world. Amen.

Leader: Ask the group to share these reflections, then ask them to read for themselves the comments in exercise 3.

2. Take a few minutes to reflect on any thoughts that might have come to your mind during the praying of the meditation couplets. Did God address you personally with a specific word?

3. Read these comments:

> Here is something worth more than a moment's notice. In meditation you enter the world of God, the Narnia behind the wardrobe of written words. You experience God's world in all its beauty and depth and mystery. Your experience in space and time becomes what John de Caussade called "the sacrament of the present moment" in a book by that title. Every moment becomes a moment of divine communication and illumination. Every little place becomes significant space for God. God's revelation can be seen even in that which is brief and trivial.
>
> But to enter the world of God you must leave behind the world of self, of dominating self-will, and of self-indulgence. John Calvin said that the key principle of holiness (in the world) is self-denial (of the world). By not seeking what is expedient to the flesh and by forgetting yourself and your own interests as far as possible, you can live in the world and die to it. As John Calvin said, "It is an ancient and true observation that there is a world of vices hidden in the soul, but Christian self-denial is the remedy of them all" (*Golden Booklet of the True Christian Life*).
>
> The work of the present moment is most effectively accomplished by submissive self-forgetting. It is not accomplished by withdrawal and detachment from everything, for then you would no longer be in the world God loves. Rather, it is accomplished by withdrawal and detachment from everything in yourself, in deference to the divine will that is revealed and recognized in even the most trivial things of the present moment.

Leader: Invite participants to share with the group any thoughts the Holy Spirit has laid upon their hearts. Then ask the group to meditate silently on the prayer that follows.

4. Pause for a moment to reread and reflect quietly on what you've just read.

PRAYER

1. Spend a moment of silence to meditate on the prayer by Thomas à Kempis that follows:

> Love eternal, my whole good, happiness which hath no bounds, I desire to appropriate thee with the most vehement desire, and the most worthy reverence. I desire to reserve

nothing unto myself. O everlasting light, surpassing all created luminaries, flash forth thy lightning from above, piercing all the most inward parts of my heart. Make clean, make glad, make bright, and make alive my spirit, with all the powers thereof, that I may cleave unto thee in ecstasies of joy.
—*The Imitation of Christ,* pp. 181-182

2. Read the following prayer based on John 17:14-16, 18 (pause for a moment of silent meditation after each verse):

> **Leader: Invite the group to take turns reading the stanzas of this prayer. Ask them to allow a brief time of silence after each.**

"In the World, While Yet Not of It"

Precious Lord, you are a hiding place for me.
You are my private retreat, my cloister.
I take hold of the horns of your altar and
    feel safe.
No one can harm me when I am thus
    secured.
I disappear into the quiet place of your
    presence
and find I can be alone there,
even when surrounded by crowds and
    noises.

I know now what you meant, Lord,
in your prayer about being in the world
    while yet not of it.
On a busy highway, in the midst of rush-
    hour traffic,
I can be in my monastery of meditation
    alone,
able to see the hazards and hear the horns
    of speeding vehicles,
yet be in a most holy place of safety and
    quiet.

I need not find a church, a closet, or a
    confessional
to experience you in close communion.
I take my sanctuary with me.
I need only direct my mind through my
    heart,
and there, Lord, you are. Always.

"In sweet communion, Lord, with you
I constantly abide."
With my mind thus stayed on you,
I am kept in perfect peace.

I will find sanctuary with you everywhere,
    Lord.
I will seek you in the city, in the market-
    place, at the job site.
I will look for you in the computer, in the
    crowds, in the stranger.
I will eat my meals as a sacrament.
I will wash my face as a baptism.
I will drink your Spirit from the public
    water fountain.
I will sit, go out for a walk,
lie down, and rise up again for the love of
    God.
Your presence I will practice without
    ceasing.
I will sleep with you and meet you in my
    dreams.

Most people will not know where I really
    am.
They will see me in the world, at my desk,
putting my hands and brain to my daily
    tasks.
But they will not know, they will not see
the prayer, the worship, going on in my
    heart.
My monastery will be invisible to them.
But you, Lord Jesus, know; you see me
because you are in the omniscient Father,
and I am in you,
and you and the Father are in me.
Indeed, Father, Son, and Holy Spirit have
    come
to make their home in me.

Praise be to you, triune God.
Praise be to you, holy Father.
Praise be to you, Lord Jesus Christ.
Praise be to you, blessed Spirit.

Jesus, you are no longer in the world.
I am in the world as your body.
But because you are now in me,
I am not of this world.
The world is outside me.
I am of you, Lord, and I desire every minute
to commune with your Spirit in the
    sanctuary of my heart. Amen.

CONTEMPLATION

1. Read John 17:14-16, 18 each day. As time allows, follow the first three steps of the discipline throughout the week.
2. Review the verses from John 17 you have memorized. Ponder each verse until it evolves into a prayer.
3. If you have been writing prayers or collecting the prayers of other believers from devotional literature, spend some time this week updating your prayer journal.
4. Read "In the World, While Yet Not of It" for personal or family devotions.
5. In a time of confession this week, ask yourself, What vices are hidden in my soul to which self-denial would be the remedy? Give these vices up to the Lord, one by one.
6. Each day, when you arise, pray the following prayer. Set your mind on the Spirit, so that this prayer may become a template—a fixed part of your thought, action, and character:

> I will find sanctuary with you everywhere, Lord.
> I will seek you in the city, in the marketplace, at the job site.
> I will look for you in the computer, in the crowds, in the stranger.
> I will eat my meals as a sacrament.
> I will wash my face as a baptism.
> I will drink your Spirit from the public water fountain.
> I will sit, go out for a walk,
> lie down, and rise up again for the love of God. Amen.

Leader: Ask participants to share their experiences with contemplation. Invite them to do the contemplation exercises every day, until you meet again. Conclude with a brief time of singing if you wish, and close in prayer.

Consecrate Me—in Truth and Love
John 17:17-26

READING
1. Read John 17.
2. Sing or say as a prayer for illumination, "Thy Love to Me, O Christ."

   > Thy love to me, O Christ,
   > thy love to me,
   > not mine to thee, I plead,
   > not mine to thee.
   > This is my comfort strong,
   > this is my joyful song,
   > thy love to me,
   > thy love to me.
   >
   > Let me more clearly trace
   > thy love to me,
   > see in the Father's face
   > his love to thee,
   > know as he loves the Son,
   > so dost Thou love Thine own,
   > thy love to me,
   > thy love to me.
   >
   > —Merrill E. Gates

3. Read John 17:17-26 meditatively—read it silently, slowly, and reflectively, looking for the two key ideas of sanctification and unification.

4. Read the following study notes.

   Jesus prayed for the sanctification and the unification of his disciples and of his soon-to-be disciples.

   Sanctification means "to be made holy." To be holy means to be set apart, unique, pure. The more something is *itself* (that is, genuine), the more holy it is. A holy tree is a genuine tree, not a plastic model. A holy man is a genuine man, not a god-pretender. A holy diamond is a genuine diamond, not a zirconium look-alike.

   The sanctifying agent that produces genuineness is truth. The ultimate truth is God's Word: "Sanctify them by the truth; your word is truth," said Jesus (v. 17). God's Word is

> **Leader: Welcome the participants. If you wish, join in some communal singing. Ask someone to read the passage; then invite the group to sing or say together the prayer for illumination.**

> **Leader: Ask participants to do exercises 3 and 4 on their own.**

both spoken (or written) and personal (incarnate). It is the truth of the Scriptures and the truth of the perfectly holy Christ who prays, "For them I sanctify myself . . ." (v. 19).

This means that Christ desires his disciples to be genuine people. He wants the real articles, not half-hearted followers; he wants radical (rooted) faith, not superficial religiosity; he wants holy difference, not unholy sameness; he wants transformation, not conformity; he wants imitation of himself, not mimicry of the culture.

Christ prayerfully equips his disciples with the truth of God, written and personal. He ministers to them in Word and in Spirit. As the disciples of Christ abide in the truth of the Scriptures and in the truth of Christ's indwelling presence, they are able to be sent into the world and to live and witness there with such genuineness, such integrity, that others come to believe in Christ through their word.

Christ also prayed for the unification of his disciples and of others who would become believers. Unification means to be made one. Christ prayed that the Father would protect the disciples "so that they may be one as we are one" (v. 11). In the unity of the divine Trinity, Father, Son, and Holy Spirit remain unique as distinct persons (three in one), yet they are consolidated in a body of love, incorporated in a singularity of purpose and action (one in three). Christ prays that his church on earth will be a family where there is harmony of spirit, of mind, and of will.

As long as we are safe in the family of God, we don't become lost like "the son of destruction" (v. 12). But when individuals try to stand apart from God and from people in the fellowship of love, they inevitably come apart within themselves. When they have no continuing fellowship in the Spirit, they experience a disintegration of being.

Several things can threaten this fellowship. One is the world's allurements (its evil). Another is the world's hatred. Another is the sacrifice of truth—a surrender of genuineness or holiness. Another is the closing of the circle of intimacy.

In the mix of the church's unity are Father, Son, and Holy Spirit. God desires that the circle of unity be expanded to include many others. God wants a family that is open and inviting, so that one day such a host of people will make up the company of the redeemed that the world will stop and take notice. The loving unity of Christ's disciples will, perhaps more than anything else, convince the world that Christ is God and that God is love (v. 23).

5. Reflect on one or more of these questions.

   a. According to this passage, what does it mean for us to be *sanctified*? How would that show in our lives?

   b. How should we be one as Jesus and the Father are one?

   c. How does Christ's crucifixion help us to be sanctified and unified?

Leader: Allow time for group discussion of these questions.

MEDITATION

1. Quiet yourself, center your thoughts on God, and repeat several times, pausing after each repetition for rumination:

   Sanctify me, Lord, in your truth.
   Your word is truth.

Leader: Invite your group to do exercises 1-3 on their own.

2. In silent meditation, hold each one of the following images in your heart, and consider what you are asking God to do for you:

   Lord, make me pure like the new-fallen snow.
   Lord, make me pure like gold refined by fire.
   Lord, make me true like a rare violin perfectly tuned.
   Lord, make me true like a straight arrow headed directly to its target.
   Lord, make me genuine like a diamond still in the rough.
   Lord, make me genuine like a one-of-a-kind individual.
   Lord, make me holy like a tree bearing fruit, as good trees always do.
   Lord, make me holy like God, who is always who God is.

3. Ask yourself, Who am I? Express to God who you see yourself to be. Describe yourself to God in whatever detail comes to your mind. Then tell God what you would like to be if you could be fully restored to your genuine self in Christ. Then, in faith, lay hold of this new image in Christ.

4. See God the Father. Praise God as Father with spoken sentence prayers.

   See God the Son. Praise God as Son with spoken sentence prayers.

   See God the Holy Spirit. Praise God as Spirit with spoken sentence prayers.

5. Now form a picture in your mind of Father, Son, and Holy Spirit in their oneness, exchanging love and communicat-

Leader: Lead the group in a prayer as outlined in exercise 4. Ask participants to reflect on exercise 5 for a few moments, then lead them in spoken sentence prayers of praise and thanks to God for one another.

ing truth with one another. With this beautiful image of God's tri-unity held before your conscious mind, call to mind those whom God has given you: family members, close friends, and your brothers and sisters in Christ. Give thanks to God for the ways they enrich your life.

6. Identify briefly the issues that have affected your unity in the church. Have you consistently dealt with each other in the truthfulness and love that characterizes all conversations in the godhead?

> **Leader: Ask the group to discuss this briefly, then lead them in a prayer of confession and supplication as suggested in exercise 7, bringing the things mentioned by the group before God's throne of grace.**

7. Do not belabor these issues, but take a moment to ask God's forgiveness. Then make a pact with one another never to discuss these matters again without submitting yourselves to God's example and without asking God for grace and truth.

PRAYER

1. Sing or say aloud the following prayer.

> **Leader: Lead your group in singing or saying these stanza together, then ask participants to pray silently the prayer in exercise 2. Invite them to conclude the prayer by joining you in reading aloud the closing paragraph.**

"When I Survey the Wondrous Cross"

When I survey the wondrous cross
   on which the Prince of glory died,
my richest gain I count but loss,
   and pour contempt on all my pride.

Forbid it, Lord, that I should boast
   save in the death of Christ, my God!
All the vain things that charm me most,
   I sacrifice them through his blood.

See, from his head, his hands, his feet,
   sorrow and love flow mingled down.
Did e'er such love and sorrow meet,
   or thorns compose so rich a crown?

Were the whole realm of nature mine,
   that were a present far too small.
Love so amazing, so divine,
   demands my soul, my life, my all.
            —Isaac Watts, 1707

2. Pray the following prayer.

"Unified and Sanctified"

Lord Jesus Christ, who has power over all flesh,
I praise you for letting me be numbered
among those given by you to the Father.
I praise you for the gift of eternal life,
which is to know you and the Father.

I praise you for the name "Christ-one"
    which you have given me.

I am profoundly convicted, Lord, by your
    intercession
that I become one with all my brothers and
    sisters in the faith,
even as you and the Holy Father are
    perfectly one.
I am profoundly convicted by your prayer
    for me,
that I be sanctified in your word of truth to
    such a degree
that the world may note the difference of
    holiness and even resent me for it.

But in my state of incomplete sanctification,
I find myself, at times, more disliked in the
    church and loved in the world.
Lord, if this means only that I am being
    faithful to you in Zion,
while being sensitive and caring to those in
    Babylon,
then there may not be much cause for
    concern.
But if it means, as I confess it sometimes
    does,
that I am being insensitive and uncaring to
    those in Zion,
while being unfaithful and compromising
    before you in Babylon,
then I ask you to continue your high-
    priestly prayer for me.

I plead with you, Lord, to consecrate me in
    your truth,
even as you have consecrated yourself in
    the Word of God.
I plead with you, Lord, to consecrate me in
    your love,
even as you have perfectly loved your own
    and those to whom your own are sent.

Lord Jesus Christ,
have mercy on me.
Lord Jesus Christ,
have mercy on me.
Lord Jesus Christ,
grant me your peace.

Christ Jesus, you have cast down the dividing wall of hostility in the church
by the glory of your cross, heavy enough to crush this wall.
Holy Father, you have so loved the world that you gave your only Son,
that whoever believes in you should not perish but have eternal life.
"And this is eternal life, that they may know you, the only true God,
and Jesus Christ, whom you have sent."

Draw me ever more, Spirit of the living Christ,
out of my divisive, unholy preoccupations,
into your wholly redemptive, uniting, and sanctifying action.
This we pray to the glory of the Father, Son, and Holy Spirit. Amen.

CONTEMPLATION

Leader: This is your last session, so ask the group to share their experiences as they have tried to follow the spiritual discipline of *lectio divina*. Encourage members who wish to continue to explore this discipline for themselves. Affirm members who don't feel that *lectio divina* is for them. Share ideas of how they may continue to grow spiritually in other ways.

Thank participants for their contribution to the group. If your group will continue to meet, be sure to agree on a time, place, and agenda for your next meeting. Encourage members during the coming week to follow the exercises in the Contemplation section. Conclude with a closing prayer.

1. As often as you can, incorporate the following little prayer into your conversations with God this week. Use your breathing as a reminder to pray and as a way of introducing this prayer into the rhythm of your life.

(as you inhale)	*(as you exhale)*
God my Father,	I wait for thee.
Lord Jesus Christ,	have mercy on me.
Blessed Holy Spirit,	breathe on me.

2. Remember Christ on the cross. As you see him there, address to him each day the following prayer summary of John 17. Pause to meditate after each petition:

   Lord Jesus Christ, glorify yourself in me.
   Lord Jesus Christ, finish your work in me.
   Lord Jesus Christ, pray for me.
   Lord Jesus Christ, keep me and guard me.
   Lord Jesus Christ, abide with me—in the world.
   Lord Jesus Christ, consecrate me—in truth and love.

3. Read "Unified and Sanctified" during one of your daily devotion times.

4. Memorize the prayer hymn "When I Survey the Wondrous Cross." Carry the words and music of this hymn with you each day.

5. Live your faith! Let the Word read, meditated on, and prayed over become Word incarnate—the Word lived! A

true contemplative is not only someone who lives in a hermitage, a monastery, or a convent. He or she is someone in whom the Word of God is acted out, in whom the glory of God is manifested in the flesh. The glory of self fades away when the light of Christ's glory begins to shine through.

6. Rest in Christ. The action of the contemplative's life is always and only the action of Christ. It is the action produced by resting in Christ. It is "doing" produced by being ready, for once, *not* to do. It is the increase of Christ and the decrease of self.

Bibliography

RESOURCES ON JOHN

Barclay, William. *Daily Study Bible, The Gospel of John*. Vol. 2. Philadelphia: Westminster Press, pp. 238-268.

Carson, Donald A. *The Gospel According to John*. Grand Rapids, Mich.: Wm. B. Eerdmans, 1991, pp. 550-571.

Tenney, Merrill C. *John: The Gospel of Belief*. Grand Rapids, Mich.: Wm. B. Eerdmans, 1972, pp. 243-250.

OTHER RESOURCES

Archimondrite, Lev Gillet. *The Jesus Prayer*. Crestwood, N.Y.: St. Vladimir's Seminary Press, 1995.

Bacovcin, Helen (translator). *The Way of the Pilgrim*. Garden City, N.Y.: Doubleday & Co., Inc., 1978.

Bonhoeffer, Dietrich. *Life Together*. New York: Harper & Row, 1954.

Brother Lawrence. *The Practice of the Presence of God*. Old Tappan, N.J.: Fleming H. Revell Co., 1974.

Caretto, Carlo. *Letters from the Desert*. Maryknoll, N.Y.: Orbis Books, 1972.

deCaussade, John. *The Sacrament of the Present Moment*. San Francisco: Harper & Row, 1981.

Foster, R. and J. B. Smith (editors). *Devotional Classics*. San Francisco: Harper & Row, 1993.

Foster, Richard. *Prayer*. New York: Harper Collins, 1992.

Hummel, Charles. *Tyranny of the Urgent*. Downers Grove, Ill.: InterVarsity Press, 1974.

Job, Reuben P. and Norman Shawchurch. *A Guide to Prayer*. Nashville, Tenn.: The Upper Room, 1996.

Peterson, Eugene. "Caveat Lector," *Crux*. March 1996, Vol. 32, No. 1, pp. 2-12.

Thomas à Kempis. *The Imitation of Christ*. New York: Washington Square Press, 1964.